6/08

1395

700

Splitting and Binding

Other books by Pattiann Rogers

Splitting and Binding

Pattiann Rogers

 Wesleyan University Press
Middletown, Connecticut

Some of the poems in this book originally appeared in: *Amelia, Crazy-horse, The Iowa Review, Michigan Quarterly Review, The Missouri Review, New England Review and Breadloaf Quarterly, The New Republic, Poetry Northwest, Raccoon, Shenandoah, Woman Poet: The South, TriQuarterly,* and *The Yale Review.* "The Origin of Order" and "The Answering of Prayers" appeared first in *Poetry.* "Rolling Naked in the Morning Dew" is reprinted from *Prairie Schooner* by permission of University of Nebraska Press, copyright 1986 by University of Nebraska Press. "The Objects of Immortality" appeared in *Pushcart Prize, Best of the Small Presses, X, 1985–86,* edited by Bill Henderson. "Before I Wake" appeared in the chapbook *The Only Holy Window,* published by Trilobite Press.

I wish to thank the John Simon Guggenheim Foundation, the National Endowment for the Arts, and the Robert Frost Place for giving me opportunities and support during the period when many of these poems were written.

All inquiries and permissions requests should be addressed to the Publisher, Wesleyan University Press, 110 Mt. Vernon Street, Middletown, Connecticut 06457

LIBRARY OF CONGRESS CATALOGING-IN-PUBLICATION DATA
Rogers, Pattiann, 1940–
  Splitting and binding.
  (Wesleyan poetry)
  I. Title. II. Series.
PS3568.0454S6 1989   811'.54   88-28065
ISBN 0-8195-2172-8
ISBN 0-8195-1173-0 (pbk.)

Manufactured in the United States of America

First Edition

Wesleyan Poetry

For the readers,
who give the gift of reception

Contents

The Next Story

All morning long
they kept coming back, the jays,
five of them, blue-grey, purple-banded,
strident, disruptive. They screamed
with their whole bodies from the branches
of the pine, tipped forward, heads
toward earth, and swept across the lawn
into the oleanders, dipping low
as they flew over the half-skull
and beak, the blood-end of the one wing
lying intact, over the fluff
of feathers scattered and drifting
occasionally, easily as dandelion—
all that the cat had left.

Back and forth, past one another,
pausing as if listening, then sharply
cutting the morning again into shard
upon shard of frantic and crested descent,
jagged slivers of raucous outrage,
they kept at it, crying singly, together,
alternately, as if on cue, discordant
anthem. The pattern of their inconsolable
fear could be seen against the flat
spring sky as identical to the pattern
made by that unmendable shatter
of disjointed rubbish on the lawn,
all morning long.

Mothers, fathers, our kind, tell me again
that death doesn't matter. Tell me
it's just a limitation of vision, a fold
of landscape, a deep flax-and-poppy-filled

gully hidden on the hill, a pleat
in our perception, a somersault of existence,
natural, even beneficent, even a gift,
the only key to the red-lacquered door
at the end of the hall, "water
within water," those old stories.

But this time, whatever is said,
when it's said, will have to be more
reverent and more rude, more absolute,
more convincing than these five jays
who have become the five wheeling spokes
and stays of perfect lament, who, without knowing
anything, have accurately matched the black
beaks and spread shoulders of their bodies
to all the shrill, bird-shaped histories
of grief; will have to be demanding enough,
subtle enough, shocking enough, sovereign
enough, right enough to rouse me, to move me
from this window where I have pressed
my forehead hard against the unyielding pane,
unyielding all morning long.

The Dead Never Fight Against Anything

It's always been that way.
They've allowed themselves to be placed,
knees to chin, in the corners of caves
or in holes in the earth, then covered
with stones; they've let their fingers
be curled around old spears or diadems
or favorite dolls, the stems
of cut flowers.

Whether their skulls were cracked open
and their brains eaten by kin
or whether their brains were pulled
by tongs through their nostrils
and thrown into the dog's dish as waste
are matters that have never concerned them.

They have never offered resistance
to being tied to rocks below the sea,
left for days and nights until their flesh
washed away or likewise to being placed
high in jungle trees or high on scaffolds
alone in the desert until buzzards,
vultures and harpy eagles stripped
their bones bare. They have never minded
jackals nosing at their haunches,
coyotes gnawing at their breasts.

The dead have always been so purely
tolerant. They've let their bones
be rubbed with ointments, ornamented
with ochre, used as kitchen ladles
and spoons. They've been imperturbably
indifferent to the removal of all
their entrails, the resulting cavities

filled with palm wine, aromatic
spices; they have lain complacently
as their abdomens were infused
by syringe with cedar oil.
They've allowed all seven
natural openings of their bodies
to be closed with gold dust.

They've been shrunken and their mouths
sewn shut; they've been wrapped
in gummed linen, corded, bound upright
facing east, hung above coals
and smoked, their ears stuffed
with onions, sent to sea on flaming
pyres. Not one has ever given
a single sign of dissent.

Oblivious to abuse. Even today,
you can hit them and pinch them
and kick them. You can shake them,
scream into their ears, you can cry,
you can kiss them and whisper and moan,
smooth their combed and parted hair, touch
the lips that yesterday spoke, beseech,
entreat with your finest entreaty.
Still, they stare without deviation,
straight into distance and direction,
old stumps, old shameless logs, rigid
knurls, snow-faced, pitiless,
pitiless betrayal.

White Prayer

For the white tail-like tongue of the echidna
Taking white sap from the ponerine ants;
For the white shadow of the shearwater
Sweeping like a beacon between the black
Night and the black ocean below;

For the noonside paddle of the prickly pear
Pressed flat against the sun, and the white silence
Of the impending scarlet call waiting
Inside the red-winged blackbird settled
Among the icy reeds; and the winter prairie
In the brain of the snow hare changing
His summer fur to white;

For the purest gift of white appearing
As an isolated parabola of light on the forest floor;
For the white mercy the dayflower gives
To roadside ditches, and the white soul of the eye
That can see its own blindness, and the white steps
Of this remembered ritual;

This is a prayer of white praying
For the white prayer buried in the green catacombs
Of bony coral filled with sea, praying for the white
Statement of pale root caught in the core
Of white spruce branches beneath the earth, praying
For the presence of itself with all the promised
Clarity of white within white. May the power
Of its recitation reflect off the seamless walls
Of its own examined boundaries and save us, for a moment,
From the white stare, the smothering fog, the albino terror,
The blankness of death.

The Voice of the Precambrian Sea

During the dearth and lack of those two thousand
Million years of death, one wished primarily
Just to grasp tightly, to compose, to circle,
To link and fasten skillfully, as one
Crusty grey bryozoan builds upon another,
To be *anything* particular, flexing and releasing
In controlled spasms, to make boundaries—replicating
Chains, membranes, epitheliums—to latch on with power
As hooked mussels now adhere to rocky beaches;
To roll up tightly, fistlike, as a water possum,
Spine and skin, curls against the cold;
To become godlike with transformation.

And in that time one eventually wished,
With the dull swell and fall of the surf, to rise up
Out of oneself, to move straight into the violet
Billowing of evening as a willed structure of flight
Trailing feet, or by six pins to balance
Above the shore on a swollen blue lupine, tender,
Almost sore with sap, to shimmer there,
Specific and alone, two yellow wings
Like splinters of morning.

One yearned simultaneously to be invisible,
In the way the oak toad is invisible among
The ashy debris of the scrub-forest floor;
To be grandiose as deserts are grandiose
With punctata and peccaries, Joshua tree,
Saguaro and the mule-ears blossom; to be precise
As the long gleaming hairs of the gourami, swaying
And touching, find the moss and roughage
Of the pond bottom with precision; to stitch
And stitch (that dream!) slowly and exactly

As a woman at her tapestry with needle and thread
Sews each succeeding canopy of the rain forest
And with silver threads creates at last
The shining eyes of the capuchins huddled
Among the black leaves of the upper branches.

One longed to be able to taste the salt
Of pity, to hold by bones the stone of grief,
To take in by acknowledgment the light
Of spring lilies in a purple vase, five white
Birds flying before a thunderhead, to become
Infinite by reflection, announcing out loud
In one's own language, by one's own voice,
The fabrication of these desires, this day
Of their recitation.

The Origin of Order

Stellar dust has settled.
It is green underwater now in the leaves
Of the yellow crowfoot. Its potentialities
Are gathered together under pine litter
As emerging flower of the pink arbutus.
It has gained the power to make itself again
In the bone-filled egg of osprey and teal.

One could say this toothpick grasshopper
Is a cloud of decayed nebula congealed and perching
On his female mating. The tortoise beetle,
Leaving the stripped veins of morning-glory vines
Like licked bones, is a straw-colored swirl
Of clever gases.

At this moment there are dead stars seeing
Themselves as marsh and forest in the eyes
Of muskrat and shrew, disintegrated suns
Making songs all night long in the throats
Of crawfish frogs, in the rubbings and gratings
Of the red-legged locust. There are spirits of orbiting
Rock in the shells of pointed winkles
And apple snails, ghosts of extinct comets caught
In the leap of darting hare and bobcat, revolutions
Of rushing stone contained in the sound of these words.

Maybe the paths of the Pleiades and Coma clusters
Have been compelled to mathematics by the mind
Contemplating the nature of itself
In the motions of stars. The pattern
Of the starry summer night might be identical
To the structure of the summer heavens circling
Inside the skull. I can feel time speeding now
In all directions deeper and deeper into the black oblivion
Of the electrons directly behind my eyes.

Child of the sky, ancestor of the sky, the mind
Has been obligated from the beginning
To create an ordered universe
As the only possible proof
Of its own inheritance.

The Favorite Dance of the Deaf and Blind Beggar

It contains the same precision of gesture
Accomplished by the morning larkspur leaning
Eastward toward light and the same rapid virtuosity
Of the darting fingerling in deep-creek sun
And the single turn of the many—in flocks
Of ricebirds, in schools of mackerel.

He understands, by his own body, the soaring
Of the sun-split leap of salmon after salmon
Through loop after loop of cascading current.
Without sight, without sound, still he knows
The complicated coordination, the passing-by,
The uniting and separating performed by the company
Of willow leaves, yellow catkins and their ribbonlike
Branches blowing together in an erratic wind.

In the closing of his hand, he recognizes
The slow folding of the dancer onstage, the same act
Sealed and completed in the rolling curl
Of the seahorse's tail. As if he saw and heard
The phenomenon from the inside out, the pattern
Of the waltzer's feet on the floor, like the design
Of a wood fern reflected in a pond, he perceives
In its immediate form.

What grace, the way he yearns for the reverence
Of a rising line of smoke which does not descend,
Which has no fall. What evocation, the motion
Of the blooming hyacinth in the motion
Of his beseeching.

Of course, he can comprehend, without speech,
The intricacies of this dance which tambourines
And drums, masks, scarves, mudras, *taconeo*,
The cabriole, the arabesque merely investigate,
Revealing occasionally the placement and position,
The circling and holding that were first performed,
Choreographed permanently in the spatial arts
Of his bones, in the cellular elegance of his blood,
In the old underlying routines of the brain,
Ten billion years before. His favorite dance
Is *this* dance in which he has always participated,
Rising, joining, even asleep, even sitting, still
And bound as he must, inside the enduring darkness
Of his unlimited silence.

The Sense God Gave

enough to forage successfully for grains
and grass sprouts in the protected shallows
of coastal marshes, to fatten further
on Yukon berries for a month in the fall

enough to thrust the head forward hissing,
raise the feathers and run full force
at weasels near the breeding grounds, to hold
the wings slightly from the body in an icy
rain to shelter the young

sufficient to be reliable sentries
in the courtyards of Egyptians, Romans
and Greeks, to pull the toy, flower-filled
wooden carts of Christian children
at Easter time, to be favorite
family caretaker of cradle songs,
to be roused on a hillside
and scattered forever
by John Whiteside's daughter

enough to nest on the wide nest
of the Arctic tundra, to be as gregarious
as the waves on northern summer bays,
to be flocks of sterling in the moonlight,
the color of fog in fog, to assume
the aura of ancient river flyways,
to assume the name
of snow

enough to be and perfectly be
(even as any saint or angel must)
the full, proliferating,
and ever-multifarious proof
of exactly that measure given

The Answering of Prayers

Because they have neither tongue
Nor voice, the iris are thought by some
Never to pray, also because they have no hands
To press together and because, born blind,
They cannot properly direct their eyes
Heavenward and, not insignificantly,
Because their god has no ears.

Rising simply from the cement
Of their bulbs, the iris have no premeditated
Motion. They never place one appendage
Deliberately before another in a series
Crossing space. How can they ever formulate, then,
A progress of thought moving from "want"
To "request," from "delight" to "blessing"?
How can they invent what they cannot envision—
A structure of steps leading from "self"
To "beyond"?

Consequently, and some may call it prayer,
They engage themselves in one steady proclamation
Which eventually becomes arched and violet
With petals, pertinently stemmed, budded
With nuance, a subtlety of lissome blades, a sound
Undoubtedly recognized by that deaf god
Who contains within his breast, like the sky-half
Of a spring afternoon, vacancies shaped
As missing floral clusters, purple-streaked
Intimacies. As rooted in his place as April,
It is *their* god who, standing hollow, precedes them
With the absence of brown-wine and lavender bouquets,
Ivory flags on grey-green stalks.

And in the unfolding act of his being filled,
As he becomes weighted, suffused with blossoms
And fragrance, as he feels his heart cupped
And pressed with the intensity of ascent,
In that act of being filled (perfect
Absolution) doesn't he surround, doesn't
He enable, doesn't he with fitting eloquence
Reply?

The Importance of the Whale in the Field of Iris

They would be difficult to tell apart, except
That one of them sails as a single body of flowing
Grey-violet and purple-brown flashes of sun, in and out
Across the steady sky. And one of them brushes
Its ruffled flukes and wrinkled sepals constantly
Against the salt-smooth skin of the other as it swims past,
And one of them possesses a radiant indigo moment
Deep beneath its lidded crux into which the curious
Might stare.

In the early morning sun, however, both are equally
Colored and silently sung in orange. And both gather
And promote white prairie gulls which call
And circle and soar about them, diving occasionally
To nip the microscopic snails from their brows.
And both intuitively perceive the patterns
Of webs and courseways, the identical blue-glass
Hairs of connective spiders and blood
Laced across their crystal skin.

If someone may assume that the iris at midnight sways
And bends, attempting to focus the North Star
Exactly at the blue-tinged center of its pale stem,
Then someone may also imagine how the whale rolls
And turns, straining to align inside its narrow eye
At midnight, the bright star-point of Polaris.

And doesn't the iris, by its memory of whale,
Straighten its bladed leaves like rows of baleen
Open in the sun? And doesn't the whale, rising
To the surface, breathe by the cupped space
Of the iris it remembers inside its breast?

If they hadn't been found naturally together,
Who would ever have thought to say: The lunge
Of the breaching whale is the fragile dream
Of the spring iris at dawn; the root of the iris
Is the whale's hard wish for careful hands finding
The earth on their own?

It is only by this juxtaposition we can know
That someone exceptional, in a moment of abandon,
Pressing fresh iris to his face in the dark,
Has taken the whale completely into his heart;
That someone of abandon, in an exceptional moment,
Sitting astride the whale's great sounding spine,
Has been taken down into the quiet heart
Of the iris; that someone imagining a field
Completely abandoned by iris and whale can then see
The absence of an exceptional backbone arching
In purple through dark flowers against the evening sky,
Can see how that union of certainty which only exists
By the heart within the whale within the flower rising
Within the breaching heart within the heart centered
Within the star-point of the field's only buoyant heart
Is so clearly and tragically missing there.

For the Wren Trapped in a Cathedral

IV

She can never remember how she entered—
What door, what invisible gate, what mistaken
Passage. But in this place every day,
The day shines as a muted mosaic of impenetrable
Colors, and during the black moonless nights,
Every flickering star lifts smoke, drips wax.
She flies, back and forth through the nave, small,
Bewildered among the forest of branchless trees,
Their straight stone trunks disappearing majestically
Into the high arches of the seasonless stone sky.
No weather here, except the predictable weather
Of chant and procession; no storm, except the storm
Of the watchdogs let loose inside at night.

Now when she perches on the bishop's throne
Her song naturally imitates the pattern
Of frills and flutes found in the carvings there,
The hanging fruit, profuse foliage, ripened
Curves. Her trills have adapted themselves
To fit perfectly the detailed abundance
Of that wooden Paradise.

And she has come to believe in gods, swerving close
To the brightness of the apse, attempting to match
Her spread wings, her attitude, to that of the shining
Dove caught there in poised flight above the Ark.
Near the window of the upper chapel, she imagines
She is that other bird, emanating golden rays
To the Christ in the river below.

Resting on a colonnade opposite the south wall
Of stained glass, she watches how the lines
Of her wings become scarlet and purple
With Mary's Grief. And when she flies the entire
Length of the side aisles, she passes
Through the brown-orange swath of light
From the Journey into Egypt, the green and azure
Of the Miracle of the Five Thousand Fed.
Occasionally she finds that particular moment
And place where she is magnificently transformed,
The dull brown of her breast becoming violet
And magenta with the Adoration of the Magi.

What is it that happens to her body, to bone
And feather and eye, when, on some dark evenings,
She actually sees herself covered, bathed, suffused
In the red blood of the Crucifixion?

Among the statues at night, she finds it a peace,
A serenity, to pause, to murmur in sleep
Next to the ear of a saint, to waken
Nested on the outstretched hand
Of the Savior's unchanging blessing.

Certainly she dreams often of escape, of reversing
That process by which she came to be here, leaving
As an ordinary emissary carrying her own story,
Sacred news from the reality of artifice,
Out into the brilliant white mystery
Of the truthful world.

The Grooming

Though your sins be as scarlet,
they shall become as white as snow.
                              —Isaiah 1:18

Under the branches of the elm
and the tall, blooming bushes of black haw,
in the wavering jigsaw of the sun,
you sit, naked on the bench, waiting.
The paraphernalia is gathered,
laid out—warm wash water in a stainless-
steel bowl, rinse water in the deeper
pail, creams, soaps, a sanctuary
of flannel and towels.

She begins, holding each foot
in turn on her lap, carefully,
as if it were a basket of sweet fruits.
Her fingers stroke, wetting, soaping.
She washes the toes, the tender part
of the sole, over the swivel
of the ankle, the swell of the calf.

A hedge of slender sassafras
beside the road sways, almost female
in its graces, as you stand and turn
and she sponges behind your knees,
around each leg (they *are* pillars),
along the inner thighs, without rushing,
to the groin, the slick soap lathered
beneath her hand, the rag dipped
and wrung in rinse water.

She bathes the buttocks next,
and to the front, your genitals,
slowly, carefully. The sassafras sway,
and off in the distance, out of the center
of the rice field, a ceremony of sparrows
appears, releases, dissolves.

Up the strict hollow of the spine,
your torso, your neck, the clean water,
ladled and poured through the disciplined
light of the afternoon, finds its way
back down from your shoulders, following
every wrinkle and bead of nipple
and joint, like rain through leaves
and blossoms of yellow poplar, into the creases
of your sex and out again.

This is the form of ablution:
your hands in her attentive hands,
your arms inside her ministrations.

Listen . . . *elbow, your elbow.*

Can't you hear, in the sound
of its name, how it has been innocent
forever? And doesn't the entire body, touched
with honor, become honorable? Doesn't the body,
so esteemed and cherished, become
the place of divinity?

The face, the hair, laved,
toweled, rubbed, perfumed,
clean, radiant—you are new,

new as high-mountain snow
not even yet seen, snow so fine,
so weightless, so pervasive, it is one
with the white explosions of the wind,
one with the tight, steady bursting
of the moon, one with the hardest
and safest seams of the night,
by which you now know and so must declare:
the soul can never be more
than what the body believes
of itself.

There Is a Way to Walk on Water

Over the elusive, blue salt-surface easily,
Barefoot, and without surprise—there is a way
To walk far above the tops of volcanic
Scarps and mantle rocks, towering seamounts
Rising in peaks and rifts from the ocean floor,
Over the deep black flow of that distant
Bottom as if one walked studiously
And gracefully on a wire of time
Above eternal night, never touching
Fossil reef corals or the shells of leatherbacks,
Naked gobies or the crusts of sea urchins.

There is a way to walk on water,
And it has something to do with the feel
Of the silken waves sliding continuously
And carefully against the inner arches
Of the feet; and something to do
With what the empty hands, open above
The weed-blown current and chasm
Of that possible fall, hold to tightly;
Something to do with how clearly
And simply one can imagine a silver scatter
Of migrating petrels flying through the body
During that instant, gliding with their white
Wings spread through the cartilage of throat
And breast, across the vast dome of the skull,
How distinctly one can hear them calling singly
And together inside the lungs, sailing straight
Through the spine as if they themselves believed
That bone and moment were passageways
Of equal accessibility.

Buoyant and inconsequential, as serious,
As exact as stone, that old motion of the body,
That visible stride of the soul, when the measured
Placing of each toe, the perfect justice
Of the feet, seems a sublimity of event,
A spatial exaltation—to be able to walk
Over water like that has something to do
With the way, like a rain-filled wind coming
Again to dry grasses on a prairie, all
Of these possibilities are remembered at once,
And the way, like many small blind mouths
Taking drink in their dark sleep,
All of these powers are discovered,
Complete and accomplished
And present from the beginning.

The Light Inside of Death

V

Surely there is a little—maybe like the light
A dark rain carries into the sea on a cold
And broken night or the light held in frozen
Seeds of sumac catching sun along the road
Where a blind man walks alone or the light kept
Beneath the protective wing of a sleeping
Angel that no one will believe in.

Surely in those great depths there is one
Small isolated fin of brilliance that belongs
To death alone (maybe its efficiency, maybe its age),
Flickering like a dim torch no one can recognize
On the opposite side of a foggy gorge, or fluttering
Like a miniature silver fan at the bottom
Of a cavern pool upon which all the concentration
Of the surrounding stones then must focus.

Or perhaps death procures its light solely
By symbiosis, being the only outer edge
Along which the earth's rim can form
Its shining crescent at dawn and the only empty
Frill against which the phosphorescent fern
Can shape the curling glow of its emerging frond.
Maybe death simply borrows the light of the chink snail's
Brain, the twayblade's will, whose presence the pressure
Of its blackness alone has made possible.

But surely death must possess that one tiny,
Intricate light created by the small certainty
Of its own name. And, darling, I know this too,
That in the moment that death comes to cover you,
Lying down carefully over your body, fitting itself
So well, forming belly to belly, matching
Its spreading fingers exactly to your open hands,

Finding its own thighs and its heart and its motion
By finding yours, in that moment, just like a flame
Catching hold suddenly in the center of a lantern
And rising then to fill the dark void of the forest
With its place, death will have no choice,
Must be transformed, illuminated, filled to its farthest
Boundaries by all the glorious sins and virtues
Of your real and radiant grace.

The Nature of Winter

Why, when the silver-red fox first took
The snowshoe hare in his jaws, when finally,
After the long chase through the snow-filled
Hollow, under the bluff, across the stiff
Bitterweeds, the hare clearing the creek, the hind legs
Of the fox slipping momentarily off the icy rocks
Into that dark rush, and the hare being clever
More than once, darting sideways, doubling back
(Oh, she was snow against the white snow, it's true,
Her black eyes the only thaw of focus visible
To the heaving fox. And she held as still
As a frozen crust of hillside until the last
Second, leaping away again), why, when overtaken
Finally, caught finally, dragged by her flesh
From beneath the cold oak root, snapped up,
The teeth like ivory nails through the ribs,
The spine, the blood muscles of the thigh, hanging
From his jaws, why did she cry out then? Irretrievably
Doomed, why should she have screamed then,
In that empty forest, in that vacant, less-than-sullen,
That paralysis of dusk?

And to whom was she calling? Who could she possibly
Have hoped might answer? Not the solid grey
And snow-blinded sky; not the high, thin-raftered cave,
The deaf structure of the forest; not the crossed bones,
The folded limbs of the brittle hardwoods standing
And breathing still, as they had breathed before;
Not the silver fox whose filled mouth growled
And hummed with the steady engine of pleasure.

The first wine-red, the startling warm violet
Steaming on the snow—maybe it was god's voice,
That cry. Only a god could have uttered it;

Only a god could have heard the lost fur and haunch
And womb and vessel and skull-scream of himself
Beseeching the icy knot, the cold predetermined
Circumstances of himself to save himself.
One chance, the shuddering of his wail,
Maybe this was his one chance quickly
To perceive and declare the divine pain
Of himself before he should forget again,
Expanding back into the tree-cracked
Horizon, the folded white distance,
Into the open black pit at the center
Of the stone, perfect satiation, into the wide
Starry stasis of himself once more.

Like God

The ash-colored toad
beside the woodpile is always all
that it is not. It is not the quick
flick of August tongue on harp-stringed
katydid tonight, because it is a lump of frigid
and paralyzed earth beneath snow-covered
leaves on a mid-December morning.
And it is not grim, hunch-backed shuffler
after roaches, for it is small slithery
black wing, unbound and weightless,
quivering, cavorting in the moonlit lull
of a spring pond. It is not the bone-dust
that it is, blown by wind through reedy
ditches and hollows but, equally, the first
microscopic swirl of its first mating
rising from a new gathering of water;
and not the spikes of its spadefeet alone
but also the lavender silks of its inner throat;
not the sweet salty red cushion of hidden
lung and heart but the pebble-covered
canvas of its outer hide; never the gold,
acid-etched study of its eye exclusively
but the gaping socket of leather
on the road as well; not the green metal
of its statue by the path, not the cool heavy
mud of its odor in the hand, not the racing
star-ridden composure of its original being
in the heavens . . . how perfectly it ceases!
how marvelously it endures! so secure
and obvious in the glorious absence of all
it is not that we hardly need the word
enigma.

Knot

VI

Watching the close forest this afternoon
and the riverland beyond, I delineate
quail down from the dandelion's shiver
from the blowzy silver of the cobweb
in which both are tangled. I am skillful
at tracing the white egret within the white
branches of the dead willow where it roosts
and at separating the heron's graceful neck
from the leaning stems of the blue-green
lilies surrounding. I know how to unravel
sawgrasses knitted to iris leaves knitted
to sweet vernals. I can unwind sunlight
from the switches of the water in the slough
and divide the grey sumac's hazy hedge
from the hazy grey of the sky, the red vein
of the hibiscus from its red blossom.

All afternoon I part, I isolate, I untie,
I undo, while all the while the oak
shadows, easing forward, slowly ensnare me,
and the calls of the wood peewees catch
and latch in my gestures, and the spicebush
swallowtails weave their attachments
into my attitude, and the damp sedge
fragrances hook and secure, and the swaying
Spanish mosses loop my coming sleep,
and I am marsh-shackled, forest-twined,
even as the new stars, showing now
through the night-spaces of the sweet gum
and beech, squeeze into the dark

bone of my breast, take their perfectly
secured stitches up and down, pull
all of their thousand threads tight
and fasten, fasten.

The Family Is All There Is

Think of those old, enduring connections
found in all flesh—the channeling
wires and threads, vacuoles, granules,
plasma and pods, purple veins, ascending
boles and coral sapwood (sugar-
and light-filled), those common ligaments,
filaments, fibers and canals.

Seminal to all kin also is the open
mouth—in heart urchin and octopus belly,
in catfish, moonfish, forest lily,
and rugosa rose, in thirsty magpie,
wailing cat cub, barker, yodeler,
yawning coati.

And there is a pervasive clasping
common to the clan—the hard nails
of lichen and ivy sucker
on the church wall, the bean tendril
and the taproot, the bolted coupling
of crane flies, the hold of the shearwater
on its morning squid, guanine
to cytosine, adenine to thymine,
fingers around fingers, the grip
of the voice on presence, the grasp
of the self on place.

Remember the same hair on pygmy
dormouse and yellow-necked caterpillar,
covering red baboon, thistle seed
and willow herb? Remember the similar
snorts of warthog, walrus, male moose
and sumo wrestler? Remember the familiar

whinny and shimmer found in river birches,
bay mares and bullfrog tadpoles,
in children playing at shoulder tag
on a summer lawn?

The family—weavers, reachers, winders
and connivers, pumpers, runners, air
and bubble riders, rock-sitters, wave-gliders,
wire-wobblers, soothers, flagellators—all
brothers, sisters, all there is.

Name something else.

The Revolution of the Somersault

The first one may have been performed underwater,
A soft green grain of jelly-seed rotating slowly,
Turning by multiple yellow hairs to place
Its cold side in a line of sun below the sea.

Or the first one may have been executed by the sea itself
Descending into its own beginning white motion
Over and over, rising again, rolling in a constant
Revelation of action with the shore.

Or maybe it was the heavens during the history before rain
That first performed the act, iris-colored
Clouds defining themselves through the outward direction
Taken by their deepest grey edges folding inward.

The top of the head pressing against the earth, the whirling
Reverse of place between hillside and sky,
Maybe this is the only way to remember
The possible loops of light contained in the recognition
Of stars, to understand how the inside of the soul
Can carry itself closest to open sun, how the circling
Of the spine can prove the central position of the heart.

The somersault may well be the very trick, the confusing
Art, the easy fall and manipulation of perception
Envied and imitated by death.

The tumbling dream of the locust tree
Fulfilled in its corkscrew pod, a blade of grass bending
With dew to meet the field-speckled damp
Of its own pure base—who can know what we know for sure
Whenever we touch the coral-colored somersaults frozen in shell
As the perfect record of the conch's life?

Rolling Naked in the Morning Dew

VII

Out among the wet grasses and wild barley-covered
Meadows, backside, frontside, through the white clover
And feather peabush, over spongy tussocks
And shaggy-mane mushrooms, the abandoned nests
Of larks and bobolinks, face to face
With vole trails, snail niches, jelly
Slug eggs; or in a stone-walled garden, level
With the stemmed bulbs of orange and scarlet tulips,
Cricket carcasses, the bent blossoms of sweet william,
Shoulder over shoulder, leg over leg, clear
To the ferny edge of the goldfish pond—some people
Believe in the rejuvenating powers of this act—naked
As a toad in the forest, belly and hips, thighs
And ankles drenched in the dew-filled gulches
Of oak leaves, in the soft fall beneath yellow birches,
All of the skin exposed directly to the *killy* cry
Of the kingbird, the buzzing of grasshopper sparrows,
Those calls merging with the dawn-red mists
Of crimson steeplebush, entering the bare body then
Not merely through the ears but through the skin
Of every naked person willing every event and potentiality
Of a damp transforming dawn to enter.

Lillie Langtry practiced it, when weather permitted,
Lying down naked every morning in the dew,
With all of her beauty believing the single petal
Of her white skin could absorb and assume
That radiating purity of liquid and light.
And I admit to believing myself, without question,
In the magical powers of dew on the cheeks
And breasts of Lillie Langtry believing devotedly
In the magical powers of early morning dew on the skin
Of her body lolling in purple beds of bird's-foot violets,
Pink prairie mimosa. And I believe, without doubt,

In the mystery of the healing energy coming
From that wholehearted belief in the beneficent results
Of the good delights of the naked body rolling
And rolling through all the silked and sun-filled,
Dusky-winged, sheathed and sparkled, looped
And dizzied effluences of each dawn
Of the rolling earth.

Just consider how the mere idea of it alone
Has already caused me to sing and sing
This whole morning long.

When at Night

Suppose all of you came in the dark,
each one, up to my bed while I was sleeping;

Suppose one of you took my hand
without waking me and touched my fingers,
moved your lips the length of each one, down
into the crotch with your tongue and up again,
slowly sucking the nipple of each knuckle
with your eyes closed;

Suppose two of you were at my head, the breath
of one in my ear like a bird/moth thuddering
at a silk screen; the other fully engaged, mouth
tasting of sweet meats and liquors,
kissing my mouth;

Suppose another drew the covers
down to my feet, slipped the loops
from the buttons, spread my gown,
ministering mouth again around the dark
of each breast, pulling and puckering
in the way that water in a stir
pulls and puckers a fallen
bellflower into itself;

Two at my shoulders to ease
the gown away, take it down
past my waist and hips, over my ankles
to the end of the bed; one of you
is made to adore the belly; one of you
is obsessed with dampness; at my bent
knees now, another watching, at my parted

thighs, another; and one to oversee
the separation and one to guard the joining
and one to equal my trembling and one
to protect my moaning;

And at dawn, if everything were put
in place again, closing, sealing, my legs
together, straight, the quilt folded
and tucked to my chin; if all of you
stepped back, away, into your places,
into the translucence of glass
at the window, into the ground breezes
swelling the limber grasses, into the river
of insect rubbings below the field and the light
expanding the empty spaces of the elm, back
into the rising black of the hawk deepening
the shallow sky, and we all woke then
so much happier than before, well,
there wouldn't be anything
wrong in that, would there?

For Passions Denied: Pineywoods Lily

Who knows what unrelieved yearning
finally produced the pink-and-lavender-wax control
of these petals, what continual longing
resulted in the sharp arcing of the leaves,
what unceasing obsession became itself
in the steady siren of the ruby stigma? That tense
line of magenta disappearing over the boundaries
of the blossom is so unequivocal in the decision
of its direction, one is afraid to look too long.

I can understand, perhaps, having a hopeless
passion for gliding beneath the sea, wanting to swim
leisurely, without breath, through green salt
and sun-tiered water, to sleep all night, lost
and floating among the stroking of the angelfish,
the weaving rags of the rays. And I can understand
an impossible craving to fly unencumbered,
without effort, naked and easily over sandstone
canyons, through the high rain of river-filled
gorges, to feel the passing pressures of an evening
sky against the forehead, against the breast.
And I can understand the desire to touch a body
that may never be touched, the frenzy to move
one's hand along a thigh into a darkness
which will never have proximity, to take into oneself
the entire perfume, the whole yeast and vibration
and seethe of that which will always remain
aloof, a desire so unrelenting it might easily turn
any blood or pistil at its deepest crux
to majestic purple.

I don't know what it is that a pineywoods lily,
with all her being, might wish for. Yet whatever dearest
thing this lily was denied, it's clear
she must very greatly have suffered, to be before us now
so striking in her bearing, so fearsome
in her rage.

The Eyes of the Gardener in the Villa of the Blind

VIII

He does it all for them—the narrow flagstone
Path carefully laid through ivory tulips,
Snow-in-summer, dwarf iris, red-tipped
Fern growing among the moss-covered rocks.
He plans the most pleasing perspectives:
Border plants—phlox and hyacinth—before taller
Varieties—delphinium and foxglove—the flowering
Quince and columns of sculpted evergreens
Positioned beyond. That yellow of the torch lily,
So beautiful at dawn against the hedge
Of purple hydrangea.

In the open brick courtyard, he tends and grooms
The spring-fed pond within which swim
The specially bred oriental veiltail and lionhead.
With thoughts of their lingering there, he prunes
The lacy mermaid weeds and nurses
The thin green saucers and violet blooms
Of the floating water lilies. He knows
They can negotiate the three wide steps
Down into the stillness of the hardwood forest,
Past the fringed orchids and rose pogonia
He has placed in the shadows near the trunks
Of the shumard oaks.

When they finally enter in the evening
Through the hinged gate, they walk slowly,
Swinging and tapping their white canes.
They hold their faces slightly raised,
Expectant, as if they believed
They could feel the designed beauty
Of that garden across their brows
Just as they feel the pattern
Of moving clouds and sun on their skin.

Aren't the white centers of their eyes
Actually affected in some way by the light
Of the scarlet larkspur which certainly
Touches them, by the brilliant rays
Of the blaze roses shining here
In this their own garden?

Can't the dark bones of their feet and hands
Assume by reflection the nurtured grace
Of the lilac bushes they envision
To be gracefully growing beside them?

Will they be able to see
The way they are there in the blossoms
Of sweet alyssum and Canterbury bell
Planted specifically for them
And among which they now walk?

How he cherishes them for the purpose
Of their presence! How they adore him
For the perfect mystery of his eyes!

Tomorrow he will mulch and cultivate
The floribunda, the field of narcissus.
He will arrange the hanging sprays of magenta
And maroon portulaca spilling over the low
Rock walls and clear the pond of fallen leaves
And weed the east ridges of columbine and sweep
The walk circling the daffodils and violas
And wait again for evening.

What the Sun God Saw One Summer Afternoon

Looking long enough, right before his eyes
he saw the sheaths of leaf and tassel
and stem split and fall, layer
after layer, like transparent skins
from around each stalk, until all the barley
and rushes stood complete and naked,
a thousand narrow blades of fire
bending and shimmering across the field.

And the smooth asters and sweet clovers,
releasing their outer shells of texture
and fragrance and color, became small perpetual
explosions poised on their glowing stems.
Without the bronze and violet paper
of their wings or the green of their appendicles
or the black beads of their heads,
he could readily identify the dragonflies
as the ignited thrum and simmer shining
over the mud flats of the lowlands.

And in the sky, he watched the red hawk lose,
without relinquishing anything, the scales
and feathers and beak of its body
until it circled over the meadow, a gliding
bird of light alone.

How could he escape knowing then,
on that afternoon, to what *bovine*
and *pepper frog* and *lichen-covered
granite boulder* had always
most resolutely referred?

This was the first gift:
that he came to see everything,
during the moment he saw it,
as steadfastly possessing the one divine
soul of his eyes. What an indispensable,
what a benevolent god! to watch,
to recognize, to thus create and bestow
such necessary majesty.

When You Watch Us Sleeping

When you see us lying scented
in our nightclothes, the patchwork
quilt wadded at our feet, coverlet
kicked aside, when you see us still
at midnight, our bare arms covered
with the moon-shadows of the hemlock
by the window, our hands latent
and half-open on the pillows by our heads;

When you come upon any of us buried
but breathing, close to the earth,
motionless as oak leaves beneath drifts
of oak leaves or curled inside silk
body-vases hanging from greasewood
and vetch or sprawled, languid
under the broad branches
of the baobab in summer heat,
when you hear us humming hoarsely
sometimes, scarcely wheezing, murmuring
like white hens at their roost;

When you watch the green anole
on the banyan, cool and slender
as a pod, the onyx grain of his eye
closed deep in green sunlight,
when you can see how he obviously
possesses in his body, even in the slack
scaly skin of rose beneath his jaw,
even in the posing net of his ribs,
even in the corpuscle of blood
at the tip of his tail,
how he possesses in his body alone
all the power he needs to rise
and declare, not merely truth,
but rapture;

The living body asleep, so great
a sum of beauty that a billion
zeroes follow it, the eyes
sealing the head so tightly
during those moments
that the infinity of possible
heavens inside can be clearly
perceived by anyone;
when you watch us sleeping,
when you see the purest
architecture of the ear,
the explicit faith of the knee,
the old guiltless unforgiving adoring
sweet momentary tremble of claim
in the breast . . .

Aren't you sorry?
Don't you love us?

The Objects of Immortality

IX

If I could bestow immortality,
I'd do it liberally—on the aim of the hummingbird,
The sea nettle and the dispersing skeletons of cottonweed
In the wind, on the night heron hatchling and the night heron
Still bound in the blue-green darkness of its egg,
On the thrice-banded crab spider and on every low shrub
And tall teasel stem of its most perfect places.

I would ask that the turquoise skimmer, hovering
Over backwater moss, stay forever, without faltering,
Without disappearing, head half-eaten on the mud, one wing
Under pine rubbish, one floating downstream, nudged
And spit away by foraging darters.

And for that determination to survive,
Evident as the vibration of the manta ray beneath sand,
As the tight concentration of each trout-lily petal
On its stem, as the barbed body curled in the brain
Of the burrowing echidna, for that intensity
Which is not simply the part of the bittern's gold eye
Most easily identified and remembered but the entire
Bittern itself, for that bird-shaped realization
Of effective pressure against oblivion, I would make
My own eternal assertion: Let that pressure endure.

And maybe this immortality can come to pass
Because continuous life, even granted to every firefly
And firebeetle and fireworm on earth, to the glowing clouds
Of every deep-sea squirt, to all electric eels, phosphorescent
Fishes and scaly bright-bulbed extensions of the black
Ocean bottoms, to all luminous fungi and all torch-carrying
Creatures, to the lost light and reflective rock

Of every star in the summer sky, everlasting life,
Even granted to all of these multiplied a million times,
Could scarcely perturb or bother anyone truly understanding
The needs of infinity.

On Being Eaten Alive

You know the most terrifying ways—giant fish,
reticulate python, saber-toothed cat,
army ants by the hundreds, piranha
by the scores. One can imagine
being scarlet in the blood
of a lion or rolled as pellets
in a wolf's belly or ossified
in the barreled bones
of a grizzly bear.

There are those who have been snatched
away without leaving a trace
into the flames (efficient bowels)
of a pine forest on fire or a burning
barn in August and those
who have been taken on rough tongues
of salt, smothered and lost
in a cavern full of sea.

I have seen others disappear
without a cry, wholly ingested,
limbs and hair and voice,
swallowed up irretrievably
by the expanding sac
of insanity.

But I like to think
of that old way, the most common
and slowest, the body disassembled,
diffused, slowly, consumed—particle
by particle, stigma, gradually, by stigma,
cell by cell—converted carefully, transfigured,

transformed, becoming finally both
a passing grain of blue above an early
evening silhouette of oaks and an inflation
of sun in low October fog, both the sight
of bladed wind in beach grasses
and the sound of singing in the wings
of desert bats, becoming as close
to itself as the smooth night skin
lining the skull, as the white moaning
conch of its own hearing, the body
becoming gradually and remarkably
so indisputably so.

Before I Wake

The turning of the marsh marigold coming slowly
Into its emergent bloom underwater; the turning
Of the coral sands over themselves and over their dunes
And over the scratchings of the scarab beetles
Turning over the dung of the desert doe; the pivoting
Of the eye of the bluefish turning inside the drawing light
Of its multiple school shifting its constellation
In the dark sea; this is the prayer of sleep
In which I lay myself down to dream.

The quiet enclosed by the burrowing wolf spider
Dragging its egg sac to the surface to sun;
The stillness covered by the barren strawberry
Making its fleshless seed on the rocky hill;
The study in the desert mushroom knotting itself
In the arid heat; the silence of the fetal sea horses
Bound in the pouch of their father; this is the dream
Of the soul in which I lay myself down to pray.

And I've asked the outward motion of the hollow web
Of the elm making leaf, and I've asked the inward motion
Of every glinting fin making the focus of the carp,
And I've asked the involution of the egg buds carried
In the dark inside the cowbirds circling overhead,
And I've asked the tight coiling and breaking
Of light traveling in the beads of the sawgrass
And the net of the sea oats splitting and binding
And splitting again over and over across the open lands
To keep me in this dream tonight through one prayer more.

About the author

Pattiann Rogers has received a number of awards for her poetry. She won the Voertman Poetry Award for *The Expectations of Light* from the Texas Institute of Letters in 1982, two awards from *Poetry*—the Bess Hokin Prize and the Eunice Tietjens Prize—and two from *Poetry Northwest*—the Young Poet's Prize and the Theodore Roethke Prize. She received a Guggenheim fellowship for 1984–1985 and two NEA grants, in 1982 and 1988.

Rogers is visiting assistant professor of English at the University of Texas at Austin and a member of the faculty at the Vermont College of Norwich University in Montpelier. She has been the Richard Hugo Poet-in-Residence at the University of Montana and poet-in-residence at the Robert Frost Place. Other books by Rogers are *The Tattooed Lady in the Garden* (Wesleyan, 1986), *Legendary Performance*, and *The Only Holy Window* (a chapbook). She was graduated from the University of Missouri at Columbia in 1961 (B.A.) and from the University of Houston in 1981 (M.A.). Her home is in Stafford, Texas.

About the book

This book was composed by Brevis Press in Bethany, Connecticut, on a Mergenthaler Linotron 202 in Palatino, a typeface designed by Hermann Zapf. Since 1938 Hermann Zapf has designed 175 alphabets for hand composition, Linotype, photocomposition, and digital laser systems. Palatino is based on Renaissance forms and was named after the Italian writing master Giovanbattista Palatino. It was introduced in 1949.

This book was designed and produced by Kachergis Book Design in Pittsboro, North Carolina.

Wesleyan University Press, 1989